Corporate Finance Cocktails

A case study on capital structures of UK retailers (M&S, NEXT Plc and Debenhams)

Jamie Fong

1st Edition (2016)

Introduction............3

Introduction

This short e-book will look into and discuss the different theories of capital structure and critically evaluate each theory and supported with arguments. From the traditional theory to the ideal world theory of Modigliani and Miller and finally the Pecking Order theory, each theory has its strengths and weaknesses. However, a conclusion on perhaps, it is the hybrid theory of the traditionalist and the Pecking Order seems to be the optimal capital structure that a company should strive for.

The company chosen for this case study is Marks and Spencer Plc (M&S), a leading retailer in the United Kingdom. Two of its main competitors have been chosen namely, NEXT Plc and Debenhams Plc. M&S is leading in terms of total assets, number of stores either locally and internationally. Despite higher revenue of £10.3bn, its pretax profit is lower than its competitor, NEXT. The share price for the company is also in the same direction and NEXT seems to have found its optimal capital structure, a well-managed debt level, strong earning and all these are reflected in their beta- factor, weighted average cost of capital, WACC value and credit rating.

Another competitor, Debenhams, despite having almost the same gearing ratio, has higher beta factor and WACC values and poorer credit rating. This reveals that gearing doesn't do exclusively influence the market value of a company. It also reveals the other important drivers in establishing the market value of a company. The company's earning, dividend payout and share buyback policy also influence the market value of the company.

Finally, we move on to suggest that in order to optimise M&S's shareholders' value, key learning from the comparison between M&S, NEXT and Debenhams is utilised. In crafting the optimal capital structure for M&S, the financial managers need to strategise not only on the business strategy but also in evaluating the types of investors the company intends to attract and tune its financial strategy in order for the company to continue to have its stream of capital and debt facility available for future positive NPV investment and ultimately, increasing the shareholders' value and wealth.

Chapter One

Is there an optimum level of gearing?

In this chapter, we will visit the theories of gearing, outline the key features and critically argue each of the theories on capital structure.

Theories of Gearing

1. Modigliani and Miller (MM)

    Modigliani and Miller (MM) without tax

    Modigliani and Miller (MM) with tax

2. Traditional Approach to capital structure

3. The Pecking Order

Modigliani and Miller (MM)

One of the most prominent papers on corporate finance ever written, Modigliani and Miller (1958) contains Modigliani-Miller 31Theorem. MM introduced 2 scenarios and the effect on the values of the company will be looked into.

Scenario 1: Modigliani and Miller (MM) without tax

Propositions 1 states that in a perfect capital market and in the absence of tax, any combination of securities and the value of the company are not affected by the choice of capital structure. Financial leverage has no effect on shareholders' wealth.

Proposition 2 states the expected rate of return on the common stock of a levered firm increases in proportion to the debt-equity ratio, expressed in market values with the rate of increase is dependant on the spread of the expected rate of return on a portfolio of all the firm's securities and the expected return on the debt.

Graph 1: MM's theory Cost of Capital against Gearing without tax

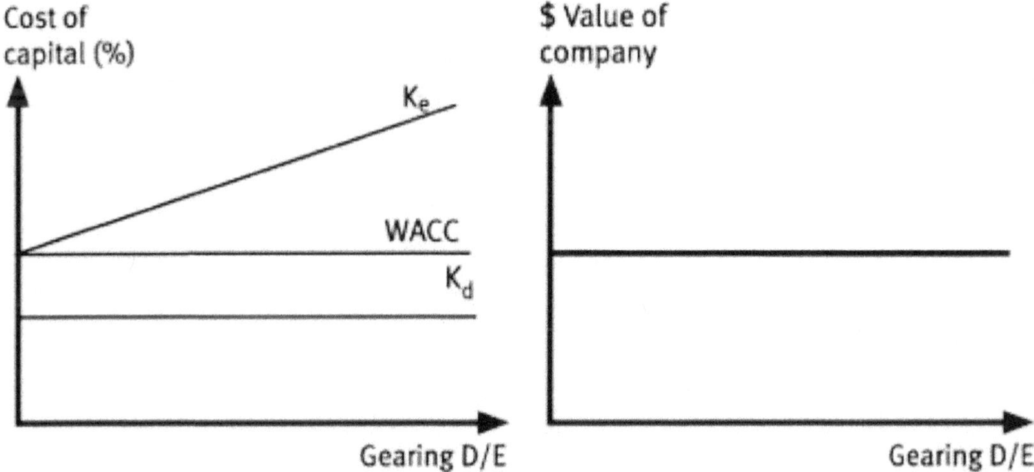

MM theory of capital structure without tax believes in the following:

- A firm cannot change the total value of its securities by splitting its cash flows into different streams.

- A firm's value is determined by its real assets.

- Disregards the factors such as flection and uncertain markets.

- Ignores the bankruptcy and agency cost, cost of writing and enforcing complicated debt contracts and taxes.

- Believes in the law of conservation of value.

- Assume financial leverage does not affect operating income and shareholders' wealth.

- Encourage firms to take as much as debts as possible..

- The value of unlettered firm is equal to the value of levered firm.

Graph 2: MM's theory Cost of Capital against Gearing with tax

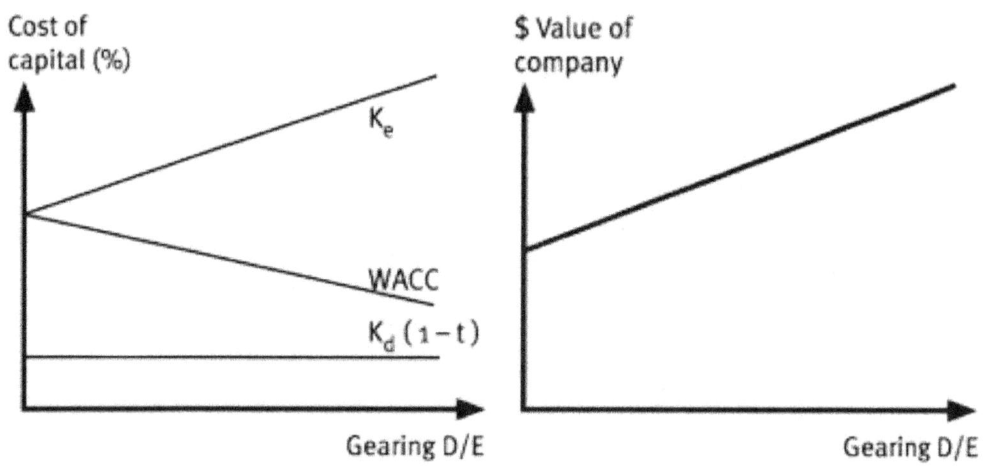

Note: Gearing is measured here using V_d / V_e

MM's theory of capital structure with tax believe:

- With a higher level of gearing, the value of WACC will fall and the market value of the firm will increase in a predictable way.

- Optimal capital structure is 99.9% gearing.

Traditional Approach to capital structure

Graph 3: Traditional theory Cost of Capital against Gearing

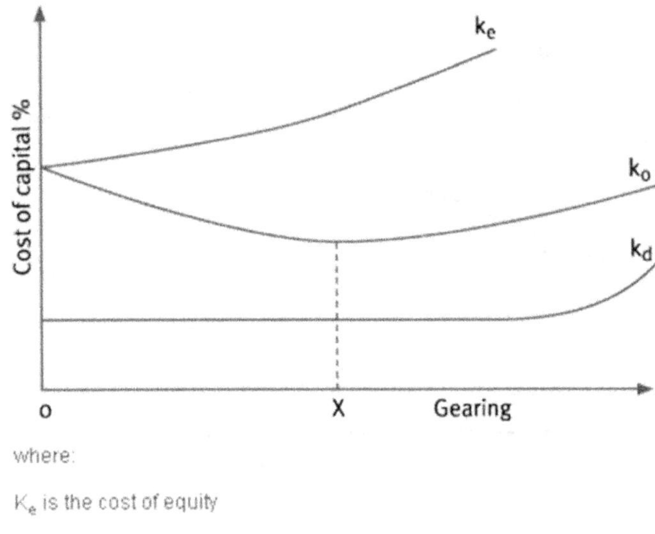

where:

K_e is the cost of equity

K_d is the cost of debt, and

K_o is the overall or weighted average cost of capital.

The traditionalists believe in:

- Weighted average cost of capital, WACC will change with capital structure choices.

- Believe that there exists an optimal debt equity ratio, X, the optimal combination of equity and debt in the capital structure of a firm which maximises its market value and minimises the cost of capital.

- On this optimal point, the weighted average cost of capital, WACC of the firm is lowest and the market value of the firm is highest.

- Once crosses this point, the cost of equity rises which will affect the WACC negatively (rises) as the shareholders have to incur higher risk and ultimately affect the market value of the firm.

- Further increase in gearing will also increase the risk of bankruptcy which both shareholders and the debtors will be worried and cause the value of WACC to rise further.

The Pecking Order

Chart 1: The Pecking Order theory of Capital Structure

The Pecking Order believes:

- Believe firms have preferred hierarchy for financing and their managers have more asymmetric information (companies, prospects, risks and values) than outside investors.

- The Pecking Order firm finances an investment with internal funds (retained earnings-reinvested), then by new issues of debt, convertible bonds and lastly new issues of shares.

- Issuance of shares is depending on timing and asymmetry information.

- Target dividend payout ratio to the investment will be adapted, avoiding sudden changes in dividends to raise internal finance.

Critical analysis on the Capital Structure Theories

MM allows a total separation of investment and financing decisions. A firm can use capital without worrying where it comes from and with MM, the assumption that if a firm uses a mix of debt and equity financing, the overall cost of capital is similar to its cost of equity with all equity financing. However, MM ignores the fact that with the new issues of debt will affect the market value of existing debts.

MM believes in the law of conservation of value- the value of an asset is preserved regardless of the nature of the claims against it where the value of the firm is determined on the firm's balance sheet by real assets and not by the proportions of debt and equity securities issued to buy the assets. This is in contrast to the view by the traditionalists and MM supported their case by showing that arbitrage will ensure that two companies which have the same characteristics except their gearing levels, will have the same overall market value.

MM assumes that both firms and individuals can borrow and lend at the same risk-free rate of interest. However, in reality, corporate debt is not risk-free and is tied to the rates of interest appropriate to government security. Although this discredits MM's proposition, it is inaccurate to assume that. The shareholders will have limited liabilities while the individuals who borrow might not but it is doubtful with the issue of debt would attract shareholders to pay a high price for a company's share. Any changes in the capital structure can be imitated by investors with the individual borrowing as they can borrow on their own easily and cheaply.

With the second proposition, MM concur with leveraging increases the expected rate of return on shareholders' investments but the risk of the firm's shares also increases. This leaves the shareholders with the same as before leveraging as the increase in risk offsets the increase in expected return as shareholders demand a higher return due to the increased risk. Again the capital structure of a firm does not affect the value of a company. Any shortfall in operating income of a levered firm (e.g: facing a recession in an economic cycle), it will affect the payoff to the shareholders and the firm's beta. Therefore, investors require higher returns on leveraged equity.

The Traditional theory shows that there is an optimal level of gearing. Despite so, there is no method other than trial and error to locate the optimal point. In response to MM's second proposition, the traditional sees as a firm increases its gearing, the holder of debt will bear some of the firm's business risk as the risk is transferred from the stockholders to the bondholders affecting the ability of the firm to further borrow and thus affecting its market value.

Despite both MM and the traditional theories believe in the financial decision of minimizing WACC and not only maximizing a company's market value; with MM's proposition 1, this is true. Even if MM's proposition 1 doesn't hold, the capital structure that maximizes the value of the company also minimizes the WACC provided that the operating income is constant. However, in reality, financial leverage can affect operating income such as the interest paid and tax shield. Shareholders are actually more concerned in being rich than investing in a company with a low WACC. On top of that, reducing WACC also encourages a logical short circuits where extra borrowing to reduce the WACC also lead to stockholders demanding higher expected rate of return.

The traditionalists believe moderate degree of financial leverage may increase the expected equity return but not as much as predicted by MM's proposition 2. Firms that borrow excessively will have their WACC declines at first but rises later. As the actual market is imperfect, firms that borrow might provide valuable service for its investors but is corporate borrowing really cheaper than individual's? Could a group of investors do better by pooling together and borrow than a firm, and saving transaction cost?

Firms that follow the pecking order theory have gearing ratios results from a series of incremental decisions, unlike the traditionalists where there is an attempt to reach a target ratio to minimize WACC. Firms in pecking order will only issue new equity as the last resort as company runs out of debt capacity and also because there are the internal and external equity. One of the main reasons why debt is issued instead of equity is how asymmetric information will influence a financial manger to issue debt over equity. Debt is issued to prevent undervalued equity when a financial manager is optimistic. If a financial manager is pessimistic, debt is issued instead of equity as new issues of equity will cause the share price to drop and the advantage of doing so is eliminated.

Instead of trying to achieve an optimal ratio as in the traditionalists to maximize its market value, pecking order firms manage their capital structure to minimize the risk of financial distress and also depending on the nature and type of industries. Firms with assets that are intangible are likely to issue common stock as bankruptcy and financial distress would be costly. Generally, due to asymmetric information, debt financing is more dominant, more frequent and unlike MM which strives to achieve highest gearing, pecking order firms believe it is better to raise equity through retained earnings than issuing stocks which can help save exorbitant issue costs and information problems.

The pecking theory helps to explain why some profitable companies borrow less not due to low target debt but because they simply don't need it. The attraction of the tax reliefs is lacking in firms that practice pecking order as compared to the traditionalists and MM. The ratio for debt will only change when there is a disproportion in internal cash flow, dividends and the need to invest in positive investment opportunities. This explains why some high profitable companies with limited investments opportunities borrow less and companies with investment opportunities but have run out of fund internally are driven to issue more debts. An inverse intra-industry relationship is seen between profitability and financial leverage where companies that invest to grow will have the investment growth rates as the industry (Ghosh & Cai, 1999). The opposite is seen where companies that are less profitable will have less internal funds and will finally borrow more due to sticky dividend payouts.

It seems being positioned on the top of the pecking order is better than the bottom as firms that have moved down the order will need external funding. The firms will rake excessive debts and shares can't be sold at a fair price causing the firms to lose good investments. Having financial slack which are cash, marketable securities, readily saleable real assets and access to debt markets, is valuable. POT firms see the market value of the company differently from the traditionalists and MM. To POT firms, a company's market value rests more on capital investments and operating decisions rather than on capital structure. To have sufficient financial slack, growth companies are lean to conservative capital structure but having too much cash can create problems too (Brealey, et al., 2006). Financial managers are likely to invest in non-profitable investment or wasting it in organizational inefficiencies, building an empire and therefore, it is suggested that having a level of debt taken to fund positive NPV projects will force a company to payout its cash and leave sufficient cash in the bank for operation. Having debt can discipline managers to be more prudent and increase operating efficiency instead of indulging in glamorous corporate lifestyle.

Chapter Two

UK Retailers

In this chapter, we will look into three retailers which are listed in the London Stock Exchange and headquartered in United Kingdom. They are Marks and Spencer, NEXT Plc and Debenhams.

Introduction

In a research by research analysts by Deutsche Bank (Debenhams, 2015), the UK market conditions and customer sentiment in 2015 were:

- Very positive UK household cash flow trends
- More cash but the same spending on non-food retail.
- Consumers have higher confidence due to high level of employment
- Consumers have greater appetite for major purchases.
- Price deflation persists in retail sales.
- Tough weather comparatives impact clothing.
- Alternative areas of consumer spending increase

Marks and Spencer Group is one of UK's leading retailers of high quality, own brand food, clothing and home products which are offered through 1,330 stores and online in the UK and worldwide. Its business in the UK which has 2 divisions, Food and General Merchandise sells high quality, great value products through its 852 UK stores and the e-commerce to 33 million customers. The food division accounts for 57% (£ 5.2 billion) of the business turnover and the General Merchandise, 43% (£ 4.0 billion) with the leading market position in Womenswear, Lingerie and Menswear.

Its e-commerce channel, M&S.COM which was launched in February 2014, puts the retailer as a leading multi-channel retailer. With over 7 million registered users, the site can cater to its changing customers' shopping habits. The weekly site visits is 6.1million, generating £ 636.5million of sales. In the international front, M&S has 480 wholly-owned, jointly-owned or franchised stores in 59 territories in Asia, Middle East and Europe which also includes the fast-growing standalone Food operation. The country-specific General Merchandise websites complemented with its overseas presence too.

The company is also committed to its ethical and environmental programme, Plan A which has 102 commitments. This program underpins everything they do. They source responsibly, reduce waste and help the communities they operate in.

In its 2014 financial year ending 29th March, 2015, the group's total revenue is £10.3 billion, a third year underlying profit falls despite increase in profit before tax of £661.2 million. The company implemented 2 crucial infrastructures in the same year. The new M&S .com website and the automated distribution centre, located at Castle Donington which are two of the largest projects of this scale in Europe. The group continues to perform with its earning per share (EPS) increases by 0.9% to 32.3p. This dividend given out was 17p per share and its trailing P/E is 13.6 (Oscroft, 2014).

A competitor for M&S, NEXT, which focuses on five divisions namely womenswear clothing, women's shoes and accessories, menswear, childrenswear and home, believes that actual physical stores possess advantages as the company continues to enjoy 5 straight years of double-digit earnings growth. Having over 4 million of active users and over 700 stores in the UK and internationally, the sales in the UK grew by 8.2% and overseas online sales increased by 61% (NEXT Plc, 2015). The company's primary objective is to deliver long term returns to shareholders through sustained growth in earning per share (EPS) and payment of cash dividends, a strategy that sees the company's EPS increased by 250% and the share price by 350%.

M&S claimed that tough conditions in the clothing market. It mentioned that there were high levels of promotional activity as one reason behind its drop is sales. Another competitor, Debenhams, a family department store, is also struggling. Although having had a few years of mixed performance, the investors' confidence is poor with its shares fell 17% which is explained as the dividend remained the same at 3.4p. The company's revenue was £ 2.9 billion and the EPS is 7.6p, less attractive as compared to M&S and NEXT.

INDICATOR	M&S	NEXT	DEBENHAMS
Gross Revenue	£ 10.3 bilion	£ 4.0 bilion	£ 2.9 bilion
Profit Before Tax	£ 661.2 bilion (+6.1%)	£ 782 bilion (+12.5%)	£ 113.5 bilion (+7%)
Earning Per Share	29.7 p (-8.6%)	419.8p (+12.5%)	7.6p
Interim and Final Dividend	6.4p +11.6p =18.0p (+5.9%)	150p (+16.3%)	3.4p (same)
Market Capitalization	£ 7.08 bilion	£ 10.63 bilion	£ 889.81 million
Business at a glance	• Sell high quality, great value products. • 2 divisions: Food and General Merchandise • M&S.com (e-commerce channel) with 7 million registered users. • Commited to Plan A	• Offer exciting, beautifully designed, excellent quality clothing, footwear, accessories and home products. • Distribute through 2 main channels: NEXT Retail (physical), NEXT Directory (online) and NEXT International Retail (physical).	• Provide customers with unique, differentiated and exclusive mix of own brands, international brands and concessions. • Offer good value at fair prices with excellent customer service. • A family department store with something for everyone. Online sales account for 14% of total sales.
Number of Stores	852 (UK) 480 (International)	539 (NEXT Retail) 180 (NEXT International Retail)	161 (UK) 87 (International)

Key indicators and business at a glance for M&S, NEXT and Debenhams

Weighted Average Cost of Capital, WACCs

In this section, we will find the WACCs for each of the retailers.

The calculations below are calculated on the assumption that the liabilities are redeemable in 5 years' time.

Risk Free Rate for UK= 1.79% based on Bloomberg Business (2016) on 7/1/2016

Equity Risk Premium for UK = 5.2% (on 7/1/2016 from Valuewalk (2015))

WACC for Marks & Spencer Group PLC (MKS.L)

Beta factor = 1.03 (Reuters, 2016) on 7/1/2016

Credit rating =Baa3 (BBB-) according to Moody's (2016)

UK Gilt 10 Year Yield: 1.79% retrieved on 7th January 2016 (Bloomberg Business, 2016)

Cost of Equity, Ke   = rf + beta factor (rm - rf)

$\qquad$ = 0.0179 + 1.03 (0.052)

$\qquad$ = 0.07146

$\qquad$ = 7.15%

Assumption made: The liabilities are fully redeemable in 5 years

UK Gilt 5 Year Yield: 1.17% retrieved on 7th January 2016 (Bloomberg Business, 2016)

Cost of Debt, Rd   = rf + Credit spread

$\qquad$ = 1.17% + 1.53%

$\qquad$ = 2.7%

Ordinary shares = 1,647.8 million (Marks and Spencers Group, 2016)

Each share market value = 530.00p (as on 27th March 2015 as the 52 weeks ended on the 29th March 2015) (Yahoo Finance, 2016)

Market Value of Equity, Ve = £ 8733.34 million

Total Financial Liabilities (non-current, interest bearing) as on 31/12/2014 = £ 1,745.9 million

Total equity and debt   = (£ 8733.34 + £ 1,745.9) million

$\qquad$ = £10479.24 million

2014 UK Government tax rate (companies with profits over £300,000) =21%

WACC   = E/V x Re +D/V x Rd x (1-Tc)

$\qquad$ = [(8733.34/ 10479.24) x 7.15%] + [(1 745.9/ 10479.24) x 2.7% x (1-0.21)]

$\qquad$ = 5.96+ 0.36

$\qquad$ =6.32%

WACC for Next PLC (NXT.L)

Beta factor = 0.58 (Reuters, 2016)   on 7/1/2016

Credit rating =Baa2 Stable/ BBB according to Moody's (2016)

UK Gilt 10 Year Yield: 1.79% retrieved on 7th January 2016 (Bloomberg Business, 2016)

Cost of Equity, Ke   = rf + beta factor (rm - rf)

$$= 0.0179 + 0.58\,(0.052)$$

$$= 0.0481$$

$$= 4.81\%$$

Assumption made: The liabilities are fully redeemable in 5 years

UK Gilt 5 Year Yield: 1.17% retrieved on 7th January 2016 (Bloomberg Business, 2016)

Cost of Debt, Rd   = rf + Credit spread

$$= 1.17\% + 1.53\%$$

$$= 2.7\%$$

Ordinary shares = 152.9 million (NEXT Plc, 2015)

Each share market value = 7,150.00p (Yahoo Finance, 2016)

Market Value of Equity, Vc = £ 10,932.35 million

Total Financial Liabilitites (non-current, interest bearing) as on 24/1/2015 = £ 838.2 million

Total equity and debt   = (£10,932.35 + 838.2) million

$$= £\ 11{,}770.55\ \text{million}$$

 2014 UK Government tax rate (companies with profits over £300,000) =21%

WACC   = E/V x Re + D/V x Rd(1-Tc)

$$= [(10{,}932.35\ /11{,}770.55) \times 4.81\%] + [\ (838.2/11{,}770.55) \times 2.7\% \times (1\text{-}0.21)]$$

$$= 4.47 + 0.15$$

$$= 4.62\%$$

WACC for Debenhams PLC (DEB.L)

Beta factor = 1.14 (Reuters, 2016) on 7/1/2016

Credit rating =Ba3 (BB-) according to Moody's (2014)

UK Gilt 10 Year Yield: 1.79% retrieved on 7th January 2016 (Bloomberg Business, 2016)

Cost of Equity, Ke   = rf + beta factor (rm - rf)

= 0.0179 + 1.14 (0.052)

= 0.0772

= 7.72%

Assumption made: The liabilities are fully redeemable in 5 years

UK Gilt 5 Year Yield: 1.17% retrieved on 7th January 2016 (Bloomberg Business, 2016)

Cost of Debt, Rd   = rf + Credit spread

= 1.17% + 3.43%

= 4.6%

Ordinary shares = 1,286.9 million (Debenhams, 2015)

Each share market value = 75.70p (Yahoo Finance, 2016)

Market Value of Equity, Vc = £ 974.18 million

Total Financial Liabilitites (non-current, interest bearing) as on 31/12/2014 = £ 197.1million

Total equity and debt   = (£ 974.18 + 197.1) million

= £ 1171.28 million

2014 UK Government tax rate (companies with profits over £300,000) =21%

WACC   = E/V x Re + D/V x Rd x (1-Tc)

= [(974.18 /1171.28) x 7.72%] + [(197.1/1171.28) x 4.6% x (1-0.21)]

= 6.42+ 0.61

=7.03%

Company	M&S	NEXT	Debenhams
WACC	6.32%	4.62%	7.03%
Gearing Ratio	16.68%	7.12%	16.83%

Graph 4: WACC against Gearing ratio for M&S, NEXT and Debenhams

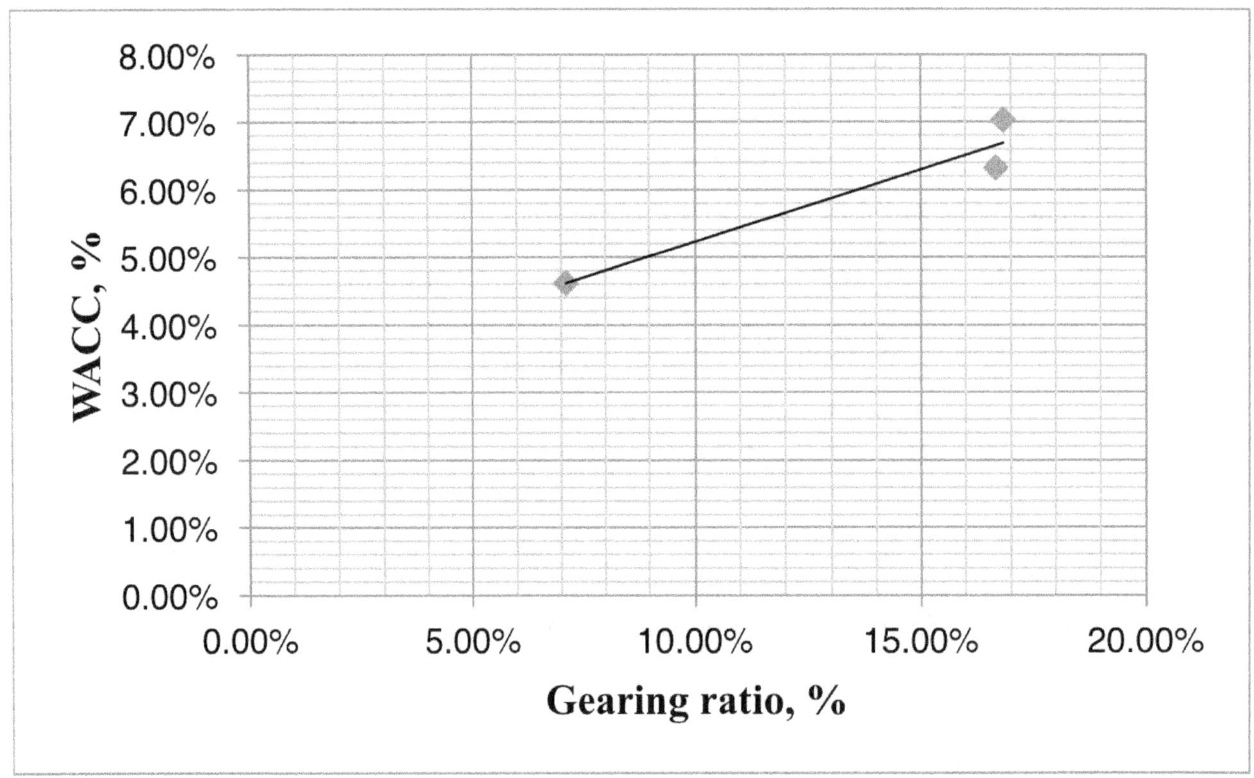

From the graph, we can see as gearing ratio for a firm increases, the WACC for a company will also increase. A company with a gearing of 10% will have a WACC value of about 5.2% while a company with a gearing of 15%, will have a WACC value of about 6.3%. Despite the fact that according to MM, increasing gearing ratio will reduce the WACC but as it is seen on the graph, the increase in gearing ratio will increase the WACC. One of the main reasons for this increase is the increase in the beta factor as the higher the gearing, the more risk it bears causing its credit rating and beta factor to increase. The risk or the expected return on a firm's assets is not affected by changing capital structure to a more leveraging structure. However, it pushes up the risk on the common stock. As a result, shareholders demand a corresponding higher return due to this increased risk.

Chapter Three

Diving into Analysis

Weighted Average Cost of Capital, WACC comparisons between M&S and NEXT and Debenhams.

In calculating the WACC value for all three companies, an assumption is made with the liabilities are fully redeemable in 5 years. As seen earlier in the graph, the value of WACC increases with the gearing ratio. As the market leader in the retailing in the UK, M&S has positioned itself with its strategic business plan. Its WACC value of 6.32% is in the intermediate when compared to its 2 main competitors, NEXT and Debenhams. NEXT has the lowest WACC of 4.62% while Debenhams has the highest at 7.03%. It is noticeable that due to the focus in creating value for shareholders, NEXT has also positions itself to have low WACC value which is achieved through its low gearing and a low beta factor value of 0.58. All three companies' WACC values are considered to be lower as compared to the industrial Cost of Capital for retail (general) at 7.22% in the US (Nyu Stern, 2016) (US data is used as the data for UK could not be retrieved). M&S has a slightly lower gearing ratio as compared to Debenhams and this has been translated into its better WACC value, beta factor and credit rating.

The beta factors for three companies are lower than US Retail (general)'s beta factor, ß at 1.16. With a lower gearing ratio, lower net debt/EBITDA, NEXT has gained itself a lower beta factor of 0.58, reflecting the lower risk perceived by the investors. In term of credit rating, NEXT again has the best rating Baa2 Stable, followed by M&S (Baa3) and Debenhams (Ba3), a reflection to each company's gearing ratio. Again, by sector in the US, the retail (general) industry has a debt/equity (gearing) ratio of 39.49%. In comparison to the industry, all three gearing ratios are at the lower end.

It is worth noting that the company's strategic planning has affected its beta factor and credit rating. NEXT has a strong focus in delivering a strong EPS which helps to raise its share price by 350% since its implementation of its Total Shareholders Returns (TSR) in March 2000. M&S has just started its programme of return of capital to its shareholders with a share buyback programme of £150m in 2014 and recalibrate its net debt/EBITDA ratio to 1.7times which is with their target of between 1.5 to 2.0 times. These have allowed the company to maintain an investment grade credit rating and continue to return any surplus cash generated to shareholders on a regular basis. Debenhams on the other hand, has a strong strategic planning for its business but is seen to have a lack of focus in improving its credit rating and beta factor through strategic financial planning such share buyback programme and increase its dividend payout to attract more investors that will ultimately drive up its share price, allowing it to reduce its gearing and improve its beta factor, credit rating and investors' confidence. This is seen as a chicken and egg scenario and will be discussed in detail in the following section.

Company	M&S	NEXT	Debenhams
WACC	6.32%	4.62%	7.03%
Gearing Ratio	16.68%	7.12%	16.83%
Beta Factor β	1.03	0.58	1.14
Credit Rating (Moody's)	Baa3 (BBB-)	Baa2 Stable (BBB)	Ba3 (BB-)
Debt/ EBITDA	1.7x	0.56x	1.3x

WACC, Gearing Ratio, Beta Factor, Credit Rating and Debt/EDITDA for M&S, NEXT and Debenhams.

Implication of Capital Structure on Shareholder Value.

Company	M&S	NEXT	Debenhams
WACC	6.32%	4.62%	7.03%
Gearing Ratio	16.68%	7.12%	16.83%
Beta Factor β	1.03	0.58	1.14
Credit Rating (Moody's)	Baa3 (BBB-)	Baa2 Stable (BBB)	Ba3 (BB-)
Profit Before Tax	£ 661.2 million (+6.1%)	£ 782 million (+12.5%)	£ 113.5 million (+7%)
Long Term Debt	£ 1.75 billion	£ 838.2 million 1.088 billion (available)	£ 197.1 million
Debt/ EBITDA	1.7x	0.56x	1.3x
Total Assets	£ 8,196.1 million	£ 2,282.3 million	£ 2,142.6 million
Total Ordinary Share	1,647.8 million	152.9 million	1,286.9 million
Share Price (according to the FY15)	530.00p	7,150.00p	75.70p
Market Capitalisation	£ 8.73 billion	£ 10.93 billion	£ 974.18 million

Key indicators for M&S, NEXT and Debenhams

From the table above, it is clearly seen that capital structure of a company affects the market value of a company. As the gearing ratios increase combine with weaker earnings, the values of WACC and beta factors increase and the credit ratings drop. Ultimately, these are reflected in the share prices and market values of the companies.

Despite M&S having a larger holding of assets, almost 4 times of NEXT and Debenhams, its profit is lesser than NEXT. This show that either M&S has not been very efficient in their management or the management of NEXT is very efficient, generating profit before tax of £782 million, £120.8 million more than M&S. NEXT seems to have achieve the ideal capital structure as it manages to reduce its beta factor to 0.58, WACC to 4.62%, achieve investment grade credit rating (Baa2 Stable) with a whopping debt facilities of £ 1,088 million available and the company's debt remains at £515m. These have been the reason that the company share price is 7,150p (as on the end of the financial year), 13.5 times higher than M&S's share price despite a much smaller amount of assets. NEXT's Total Shareholders Returns (TSR) is certainly a strategy that has proven to be functional as the company's share price has been trailing the EPS since its implementation, increasing its shareholders' value and wealth.

Graph : Underlying EPS and Share price for NEXT.

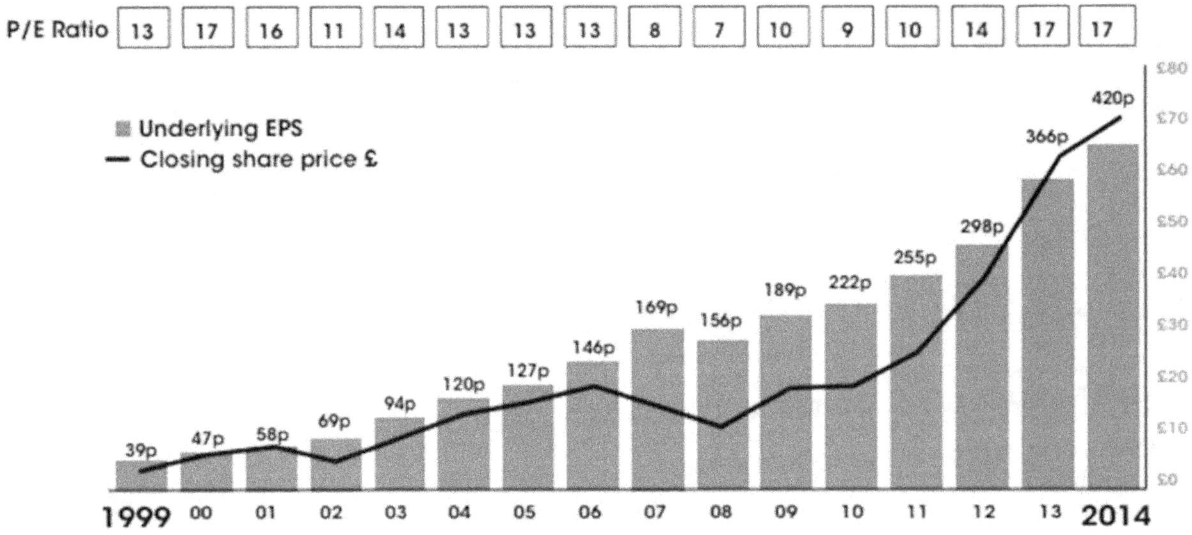

Perhaps for the same reason, M&S has started its own programme of share buyback with the recent year amounting £150m emulating NEXT. The company now practices a policy of progressive dividend policy with dividends covered twice by earnings. 2014 was a strong year for retail industry in the UK (growth or maturity in economic cycle) with all three companies able to generate strong cash flow and thus enabled them to reduce outstanding debts. M&S, with its Resource Planning System, has increased the company's cash flow from £427.9m to £524.2m, reducing its debt by £240.4m to £2.2 billion. Debenhams is also intending to adopt a progressive dividend policy.

With M&S and Debenhams having gearing ratios in almost the same range; M&S (16.68%) and Debenhams (16.83%), there is a gap between both WACCs with M&S having better values at 6.32% and a credit rating of Baa3 while Debenhams has a WACC value of 7.03% and Ba3 credit rating. Here, we can see that gearing ratio is not the only reason for the difference in WACC but it is the credit rating and the beta factor. Directly affecting the values of beta factors and credit rating is the earnings. With almost 6 times higher in profit before tax and a higher amount of assets have contributed to a lower beta factor and better credit rating for M&S despite the company has a much higher net debt/EBITDA ratio of 1.7x than Debenhams at 1.3x and total debt of £2.2 billion, 6.9 times higher than Debenhams's (£319.8m). This has prevented Debenhams from getting a fair price for its shares risking future access to capital for future development, dimming its shareholders' value.

The key concern here will be the earnings and total cash flow of the company (Ross, 88). The profit before tax for Debenhams of £113.5 million (net debt/EBITDA of 1.3x) is seen by the market as low. In retails, any drop in the economy will directly affect company's revenue, risking the company into debt default and higher risk for bankruptcy. The same is seen in M&S. However, with earning of £661.2 million, M&S is seen to have better capability in repaying its debt. NEXT however has an earning higher than its debt, a major boost of confidence to its investors. Again, this has brought positive result to its market value. Perhaps, other than gearing, the ratio of debt to earning is equally important in increasing shareholder's value. The management of the company needs to invest more prudently in a higher positive NPV development.

It is worth noticing if MM propositions were realistic, they are certainly not shown in all three companies. In MM, the gearing of a company does not affect its WACC and the market value but it is shown otherwise in all three companies. Gearing ratios, earnings and assets influence the beta factors, WACCs, credit ratings and ultimately, the share price and market values. It seems that the traditionalist theory is valid here for NEXT, having found its optimal capital structure, sees its share price increases over the years reflecting the investors' confidence in the firm or perhaps its practice in the Pecking Order Theory.

It is also clearly shown that the Pecking Order Theory is valid in all three companies with all three believe in using their existing cash flow to fund any investment and expansion and try to reduce their amount of debt. M&S has reduced its debt as mentioned earlier and Debenhams has also repurchased £25.0 million of the £225.0 million senior notes and cancelled £75.0 million of the £425.0 million revolving credit facility. These practices are in contrast to MM where based on the theory, companies should increase gearing for higher tax saving. Perhaps, in an effort to increase the firms' market values, having a high gearing despite the tax advantage is seen as an obstacle. This is true as having higher gearing not only sees the beta factor, WACC and credit rating suffer but also the future possibilities of securing debt and also the incremental cost of debt that comes with each of the debt issuance

Most of the companies instead of issuing more shares, repurchase its own shares and refund any surplus to their shareholders. NEXT generated £363m of surplus cash after capex, interest, ordinary dividend and tax in the financial year and returned £361m of this to the shareholders through special dividends of £223m and share buybacks of £138m. In fact, the company will continue to buy back its own shares provided it fits the criteria set out. NEXT uses the concept of Equivalent Rate of Return (ERR) with the minimum ERR set at 8% for a return in equity investments. The company uses their profit before tax as guidance and the current new upper limit for buybacks of £ 68.27. The company will only buy back its shares if their share price remains above the maximum limit. Share buyback is normally a good signal that the financial manager of the company is confident with its own company, revealing some of the asymmetric information of the company. Choosing to payout dividends (tax heavy) and at the same time share buybacks (lower tax), NEXT has captivated both types of investors, the conservative (right) and the left who believe higher dividend payout reduces the company value. Whichever it is, the increasing share prices over the year tell that the investors are happy with the policy.

In the quest to explain how a firm manages its capital structure, it seems having financial slacks (cash, marketable securities, readily saleable real assets and access to debt markets) should be the target of each company in order to maximize the shareholders' wealth and value. Debenhams tries to increase its shareholders' value by implementing a strategy with its first priority for cash in Debenhams is to invest in the company's strategy to build a leading international, multi-channel brand followed by paying the shareholders a dividend and finally, achieving a new medium-term target for net debt/ EBITDA of 0.5 times instead of 1.0 previously. These sacrifices the shareholders' wealth, stripping the capital value of the share price as other investors start to view the shares as less attractive due to lower dividend payout compared to other competitors or perceive the company is building an empire, sacrificing the shareholders' wealth. This will put strain on its credit rating as well and possible future growth will be on the stake. A right balance between the relationship of a company's vision and its investors is crucial. Financial managers need to craft a capital structure that will enable the companies to have financial slacks and allow the companies to continue to have the fund for positive NPV investment and grow.

M&S is heading the right direction. The company has increased its interim dividend by 3.2% with further 7.4% increase in the final dividend attracting the investors who are clamoring for higher payout. With the strategic plan of funding future growth through its existing cash flows, being committed to a strong balance sheet to maintain an investment grade credit rating and returning any surplus cash generated to shareholders on a regular basis, this will propel the company's market value. NEXT has done it right by having a centralized treasury function which manages its liquidity, interest and foreign currency risks to manage and mitigate the risk of not having financing facilities. M&S has implemented its own Resource Planning System which has increased the company's cash flow this year. Certainly, a more agile financial management is needed to capture the ever changing business environment and appetite of the shareholders and investors.

Pecking Order theory seems to be very dominant among the three companies. However, with NEXT having found its optimal capital structure, perhaps, it is the hybrid theory of the traditionalist and the Pecking Order that M&S financial managers should strive for. M&S has to strategize which types of investors they want to attract; those preferring high dividend payout (increase the return in shareholders' pocket but at the same time high tax) such as pension funds or tax-exempt institutions or share buybacks (returns in the form of capital gains) investors such as highly-taxed individuals and merge it into their business and financial strategies in order to maximize the company's fullest potential and value within the firm's lifecycle (Bulan & Zhipeng, 2009). With Plan A, it seems M&S is looking for long-term sustainable investors that will value its propositions.

Chapter Four

Conclusion

Crafting the ideal capital structure for a company is like preparing a perfectly balanced cocktail. Apart from the variety types of cocktails available, getting the right composition of ingredients, temperature and presentation require so much science, not to mention the personal preference of each of its drinkers. The same goes to a capital structure of a company. The need for the right gearing attuned to the nature of its business, the environment, the economic cycle of the firm, industry and country and all its stakeholders is important. Trials and error through the traditionalist way of finding the optimal level of gearing, to the ideal world of MM and finally the Pecking Order Theory, financial managers strive to find the essence in the hope to increase the shareholders' value. M&S and its 2 main competitors, NEXT and Debenhams seem to be moving toward the hybrid theory of traditionalist and the Pecking Order Theory as they strive to increase their shareholders' value.

Bibliography and References

Bloomberg Business, 2016. *UK Gilt Yields.* [Online]
Available at: http://www.bloomberg.com/markets/rates-bonds/government-bonds/uk
[Accessed 7 January 2016].

Brealey, R. A., Myers, S. C. & Allen, F., 2006. *Corporate Finance.* Eighth ed. New York: McGraw Hill.

Bulan, L. & Zhipeng, Y., 2009. The Pecking Order Theory and the Firm's Life Cycle. *Banking& Finance Letters,* 1(3), pp. 129-140.

Damodaran, A., 2001. *Corporate Finance; Theory and Practice.* Second ed. New Jersey: John Wiley & Sons, Inc.

Debenhams Plc, 2015. *DEBENHAMS PLC - FULL YEAR RESULTS.* [Online]
Available at: file:///C:/Documents%20and%20Settings/user/My%20Documents/Downloads/Debenhams%20plc%20RNS%20221015.pdf
[Accessed 7 January 2016].

Debenhams, 2015. *2015 Annual Report,* London: Debenhams Plc.

Ghosh, A. & Cai, F., 1999. Capital Structure: New Evidence of Optimality and Pecking Rder Theory. *American Business Review,* 17(1), pp. 32-39.

Marks and Spencers Group, 2016. *2015 Anuual Report,* London: Marks and Spencer.

Moody's, 2014. *Rating Action: Moody's assigns Ba3 rating to Debenhams plc; outlook stable.* [Online]
Available at: https://www.moodys.com/research/Moodys-assigns-Ba3-rating-to-Debenhams-plc-outlook-stable--PR_302037
[Accessed 7 January 2016].

Moody's, 2016. *Marks and Spencers Plc.* [Online]
Available at: https://www.moodys.com/credit-ratings/Marks-Spencer-plc-credit-rating-463500
[Accessed 7 January 2016].

Moody's, 2016. *NEXT Plc.* [Online]
Available at: https://www.moodys.com/credit-ratings/NEXT-plc-credit-rating-2990
[Accessed 7 January 2016].

NEXT Plc, 2015. *2015 Annual Report,* Leicester: NEXT Plc.

Nyu Stern, 2016. *Cost of Capital by Sector (US).* [Online]
Available at: http://pages.stern.nyu.edu/~adamodar/New_Home_Page/datafile/wacc.htm
[Accessed 7 January 2016].

Oscroft, A., 2014. *Marks and Spencer Group Plc Falling Behind The Competition.* [Online]
Available at: http://www.fool.co.uk/investing/2014/05/20/marks-and-spencer-group-plc-falling-behind-the-competition/
[Accessed 28 December 2015].

Reuters, 2016. *Debenhams Plc.* [Online]
Available at: http://www.reuters.com/finance/stocks/overview?symbol=DEB.L
[Accessed 7 January 2016].

Reuters, 2016. *Marks and Spencers Group Plc.* [Online]
Available at: http://www.reuters.com/finance/stocks/overview?symbol=MKS.L
[Accessed 7 January 2016].

Reuters, 2016. *NEXT Plc.* [Online]
Available at: http://www.reuters.com/finance/stocks/overview?symbol=NXT.L
[Accessed 7 January 2016].

Ross, S., 88. Comment on the Modigliani-Miller Propositions. *Journal of Economic Perspectives,* 2(4), pp. 127-133.

Valuewalk, 2015. *Market Risk Premium & Risk-Free Rate Used For 41 Countries In 2015.* [Online]
Available at: http://www.valuewalk.com/2015/05/market-risk-premium-risk-free-rate-used-for-41-countries-in-2015/
[Accessed 7 January 2016].

Yahoo Finance, 2016. *Debenhams PLC (DEB.L).* [Online]
Available at: https://uk.finance.yahoo.com/q/hp?a=&b=&c=&d=0&e=17&f=2016&g=d&s=DEB.L%2C+&ql=1
[Accessed 7 January 2016].

Yahoo Finance, 2016. *Marks & Spencer Group PLC (MKS.L).* [Online]
Available at: https://uk.finance.yahoo.com/q/hp?s=MKS.L
[Accessed 7 January 2016].

Yahoo Finance, 2016. *Next PLC (NXT.L).* [Online]
Available at: https://uk.finance.yahoo.com/q/hp?a=&b=&c=&d=0&e=17&f=2016&g=d&s=NXT.L%2C+&ql=1
[Accessed 7 January 2016].

About Jamie Fong

Jamie is a professional passionate in corporate finance. Having completed her MBA and more papers related to corporate finance, regulatory and leading a company from the finance perspective, she believes she can add values to an organization. Experienced in language analysis, she has transferred her analytical skills into numbers. She simplifies anything that is complex and makes it intuitive.

About Corporate Finance Cocktails

This short e-book is a product of intensive research that has incorporated corporate finance perspectives from a wealth of sources and uses real-life companies to enhance learning. As the data taken into analysis were compiled in the early of 2016, some of information might not reflect current situation in the organisations studied. The material has been prepared for general information purposes only and is not intended to be relied upon accounting, tax, or other professional advice. Please refer to your advisors for specific advice.